GOD
AND
PIZZA

A TESTIMONY IN FAITH, HOPE, AND LOVE FOR JESUS CHRIST AND USING THE POWER OF PRAYER IN LIFE AND BUSINESS!

JACK J MARTINO

Trilogy Christian Publishers
A Wholly Owned Subsidiary of Trinity Broadcasting Network
2442 Michelle Drive
Tustin, CA 92780
Copyright © 2024 by Jack J. Martino
All Scripture quotations, unless otherwise noted, taken from THE HOLY BIBLE, NEW INTERNATIONAL VERSION®, NIV® Copyright © 1973, 1978, 1984, 2011 by Biblica, Inc.® Used by permission. All rights reserved worldwide.
All rights reserved, including the right to reproduce this book or portions thereof in any form whatsoever.
For information, address Trilogy Christian Publishing
Rights Department, 2442 Michelle Drive, Tustin, CA 92780.
Trilogy Christian Publishing/ TBN and colophon are trademarks of Trinity Broadcasting Network.
For information about special discounts for bulk purchases, please contact Trilogy Christian Publishing.

Trilogy Disclaimer: The views and content expressed in this book are those of the author and may not necessarily reflect the views and doctrine of Trilogy Christian Publishing or the Trinity Broadcasting Network.

10 9 8 7 6 5 4 3 2 1
Library of Congress Cataloging-in-Publication Data is available.
ISBN 000-0-0000-0000-0
ISBN 000-0-0000-0000-0 (ebook)

GOD AND PIZZA

A testimony in faith, hope, and love for Jesus Christ by using the power of prayer to change your life and business in ways you cannot even imagine!

Bonus material: Pizza recipes for you to enjoy with family and friends!

Author Jack J. Martino

DEDICATION

To my mom who is in heaven seated at God's table, thank you for being my mom! To my dad for teaching me discipline and the skills of life!

To my children Joseph and Marissa, who inspire me and make me so proud to be their father!

To Jesus Christ for his love, strength, and guidance in my life!

INTRODUCTION

Hello, my name is Jack J. Martino.

What you're about to read is the story of my life before and after I discovered the importance of the power of prayer and knowing that God sent his only begotten son Jesus Christ to be a living sacrifice on the cross and shed his blood to forgive us of all our sins.

Let me start by telling you about my history. I was born in Brooklyn, New York to my loving parents, Joseph and Francis Martino. I am the second child and only son of four siblings. My parents were of the Catholic faith, so as an infant I was baptized. In grammar school I received communion and in middle school I received confirmation. We went to church every Sunday morning. I knew Jesus was an important person because Mom proudly displayed beautiful pictures of him around the house, but I had not yet understood what he had done for me.

I had a happy childhood and a family full of love. My father had four brothers and one sister so there were lots of aunts, uncles, and cousins to spread that love around. We always had fun on our trips to Long Island to visit our family.

My father had all kinds of odd jobs. He was a butcher, a baker, an ice cream man, and a shoe repair man! My father was hardworking and did whatever he could to support his family. Eventually, he opened his first pizza shop in Huntington, New York at the advice of his older brother, my uncle Sal. This is when I first experienced working in the pizzeria business as a 12-year-old boy.

In this book, I share my personal story of how using the power of prayer and having faith, hope, and love for Jesus Christ gives you success in everything you do!

Whether in your business, your family, or your day-to-day life, call upon God and our Lord Jesus Christ to walk with you. Pray for Jesus to walk in front of you for guidance, walk behind you for direction, and walk on the left and right for balance! If you truly believe,

I can guarantee he will give you peace, success, and happiness.

TABLE OF CONTENTS

Chapter I: In the Beginning 11

Chapter II: Following God's Plan for My Life! 15

Chapter III: The Prodigal Son Returns Home! 19

CHAPTER IV: Invite God to be with You
Every Step of the Way! 23

Chapter V: Seek God's Advice in Every Situation! 25

Chapter VI: Always Please God and Set Goals! 27

Chapter VII: You Will Have Your Ups and Downs! 29

Chapter VIII: Thanking God and Giving Back! 31

Chapter IX: Remembering What God
Has Done for You! 33

Chapter X: Let Them Eat with Their Eyes! 37

Chapter XI: Teaching the Next Generation! 41

Chapter XII: Have Patience with God and People! 43

Chapter XIII: Find Time to Make God
and Yourself Happy! 45

Chapter XIV: Conclusion: Be Grateful 49

Chapter XV: A Business Plan 51

Chapter XVI: Pizza Recipes 55

Conclusion 67

CHAPTER 1:

IN THE BEGINNING

My parents purchased a two-story home on Long Island in the town of West Babylon, where I attended high school. Soon, I started working at my father's pizzeria. Every Friday after school, my mother would drop me off and I would work the night shift and all-day Saturday. I enjoyed working and learning side by side my father as he taught me the basics about the pizza business. My father was an old school businessman of Sicilian descent. He was a serious and strict man, and he was a little hard on me! Not all the time, of course, but when I needed him to be. I only now appreciated what he taught me.

He used to say to me, "You start at the bottom and work your way up!" I thought, *Wait, you own this business and I'm your son! I have to start at the bottom?* But I wouldn't say that out loud. So, he first showed me how to wash dishes and mop the floors. "You start here give it your all and when you get it right, go teach someone else how to do that job!" he told me. Even though I questioned him internally,

I was still so excited to be there that I didn't mind how hard I was working. Once I got good at it, I taught someone else to wash the dishes and mop the floors.

Then my father came to me and said, "Now I will show you how to prepare the dough, sauce, mozzarella cheese, and pizza toppings." I enjoyed that job very much because I knew I was getting closer to making pizza! Once again, when I mastered preparing the pizza ingredients, I taught someone else how to do it.

By then, I started feeling pretty good about myself. I couldn't wait for the day my father would teach me how to make pizza! I used to watch him for hours as he would spin the dough in the air and catch it in his hands, looking cool and confident as the flour puffed out like a cloud of smoke. That's the job I really wanted to learn. Eventually, the day came when my father told me it was time! I was so excited to learn that I could hardly wait to go to the pizzeria after school. That Friday, my father finally taught me the proper way to make a great pizza.

It was great working with my father. I really got to know him better as a person, and I found out he was a hardworking man with a great sense for business. I enjoyed that time in my life. As a teenage boy, I really enjoyed the money I was earning too. When I graduated from high school, I decided to work for my father full-time. That meant long hours, usually sixty-to-seventy-hour weeks. However, I did not mind the crazy hours I was working because I really enjoyed what I was doing. As time passed, my father started teaching me how to run the pizzeria. He taught me how to do inventory, payroll, deposits, and how to balance a checkbook. I learned what I could from my father in the pizza business and appreciated every single moment, but I felt that I needed to go out on my own. By the time I was 25 years old, I was able to save up some money and decided to go to Florida to open my own pizzeria! Why I thought that Florida was the best place to go? Well, I just felt like I was lead there! I believe now that God was speaking to me in a soft, still voice. Even though it was hard to leave everything and move 1100 miles away to start a new life, I knew I had to go!

> *"But if from there you seek the Lord your God, you will find Him if you seek Him with all your heart and with all your soul."*
> **Deuteronomy 4:29**

CHAPTER II:

FOLLOWING GOD'S PLAN FOR MY LIFE!

When I arrived in Florida, I settled in a small town called Deltona. I didn't know anyone except for my cousin! He had heard from a friend that there was a pizzeria restaurant for sale. After we went to see the place and met the owners, we made an offer and opened our own restaurant.

In the beginning, things were going pretty well. At that moment, I thought I had made it. I finally had my own place, and I thought we were going to be successful. I realize now that I had no structure, and I didn't have God in my life to guide me. Eventually, my cousin, whose father also had a pizzeria, started disagreeing with me on how we should run our business. He had his ways he learned from his father, and I had mine. Eventually, things didn't work out. I sold my half of the business to him, and we parted ways. I found myself alone in Florida with no business and no income.

I could have crawled back to Long Island to work for

my father again, but I had an urge to stick around. Soon, I met a gentleman who owned a local shopping center outside of Deltona, and he was willing to rent me a space to open a pizzeria! I was so excited that I called up my father to tell him all about it. He was excited for me too, but I could hear a little sadness in his voice. I knew he would rather have me come home.

But, after the call, I couldn't wait to get started. Upon signing the lease and going through the process of starting the pizzeria, the landlord invited me to come over to his house and have dinner with his family. *I just met this man, and now he's inviting me over for dinner?* I was happy and appreciative. He introduced me to his wife and two sons and instantly I felt like they were family. His wife made dinner: pasta with tomato sauce and meatballs, fresh Italian bread, and an antipasto salad. The aroma in the kitchen was amazing and reminded me of home. After dinner, we started talking and getting to know each other better. They ask me to attend their Christian church that upcoming Sunday and I said I would love to. I had no idea what Christianity was all about after all, and this family was so kind and loving I was excited to learn. As I started to get the pizzeria ready, the landlord and his sons went out of their way to help me lay down tile floors, put up counters, install equipment, and paint the walls. That's how I learned how God will send good people to help fulfill your destiny. I couldn't believe how nice they were to me, yet I knew it was their love for God. That's where I found the Holy Spirit and the love of Jesus Christ.

I opened the pizzeria and business started off slowly. I was doing everything I knew to make it a success by working hard, but I wasn't praying for God's presence and for Him to lay His hands on and bless my business. Ultimately, the pizzeria failed. Feeling like a complete failure, I sold the restaurant and returned to Long Island, wondering, *Will my father welcome me back to work at his pizzeria restaurant?*

"Devise your strategy, but it will be thwarted. Propose your plan, but it will not stand, For God is with us."
Isaiah 8:10

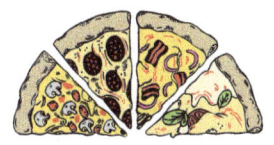

CHAPTER III:

THE PRODIGAL SON RETURNS HOME!

When I returned home to Long Island, I couldn't wait to be baptized and call on the Holy Spirit to give divine substance to my life. I started attending the local Christian church where I was water baptized and gave my life to Jesus! That's when I realized I can do all things because He is with me. I remember the day I arrived, my mother and father greeted me with joy and love. My father told me he was so happy I decided to come home and help him at his pizzeria. My mother cooked me a beautiful and delicious lasagna knowing that was my favorite dish. I felt so welcomed and loved. I knew this was my home.

In the time I was gone, my father purchased a new pizzeria restaurant which was much bigger than the original in Huntington. This one was in Hauppauge, New York. After dinner, my parents and I started talking about what my position would be at this pizzeria.

I wanted to learn more about this business. I wanted experience!

At this location I learned about the business side of pizzerias, which really sharpened my skills. I knew every step in building and running a business more efficiently. However, I still needed the spiritual knowledge it takes to run a business. I started reading the Bible and studying the Word. I began faithfully attending a Christian church to continue studying and understanding that how God works in your life. I learned how He will give me the strength, wisdom and knowledge in building a business by giving it to the Lord. Having dedicated my business to Him, I knew I could do no wrong!

Upon taking over the restaurant, my father and I decided to completely renovate it from top to bottom. I added new Italian pasta dishes, dinner entrees, and even introduced gourmet style pizza. With my dedication and love for God, I was able to build up that business in three years; increasing sales exponentially.

Things were going great. I even fell in love with a beautiful woman who worked there as a waitress. We got married, and a few years later had two beautiful children. My mother and father were so happy and proud of me! I was on top of the world.

However, I forgot who really made this all possible. I was acting like I did it all on my own. Things in my life started getting shaky, and I lost control. I let the success I was experiencing get to me. I stopped praying, giving God the glory, and going to church. Life was getting difficult. I started feeling lost, and I watched the business slowly slip out of my hands.

Eventually, in 2014, we had to sell it. That's when I realized the business failed because I lost faith and stopped praying. It wasn't because of how I was running the business; it was because of how I was not praying, thanking God for what he had given me, and calling down blessings. Knowing I failed everyone that believed in me; my mother, my father, my wife, and my children, I fell to my knees and asked God for forgiveness.

"Please God, I'm sorry for thinking it was all me! I know now it was all you that gave me the strength to accomplish everything! Please forgive me!" I prayed. I started attending church again, I started praying again, and I started feeling that peace and love again! As time passed, I knew I was connecting with God and felt His forgiveness.

Eventually, I found another location for a pizzeria, and I prayed and prayed again. I asked God to be by my side throughout that whole process. I told Him, "I'm going to dedicate this business to you, God, and the Lord Jesus Christ. I will give you my all. I'm going to do whatever I can to build his business with the skills and the knowledge that you've given me!"

And I did. I decided to worship and praise His holy name every day by playing Christian music on the music system in the restaurant, even when people were telling me I shouldn't. I wanted to worship and praise Jesus all day long! I soon realized that people actually enjoyed it. They were searching for some hope, faith, and love of their own. I gave my all to God in the way I treated people with respect and kindness. I tried to run my business and take care of my customers with patience and the love of God.

Trust God, use the power of prayer, and dedicate your business and your life to the Lord every day. Pray for success, pray for health, pray for love, and you will receive it! As Jesus says, "I will do whatever you ask in my name, so that the Father may be glorified in the son," (John 14:13).

> *"But when you ask, you must believe and not doubt, because the one who doubts is like a wave of the sea, blown and tossed by the wind."*
> **James 1:6**

CHAPTER IV:

INVITE GOD TO BE WITH YOU EVERY STEP OF THE WAY!

The biggest mistake I made was not inviting God into my life and asking for His strength, knowledge, and guidance to show me the path to opening a business. I believe it's important to ask Him to walk with you and show you the way. He gives you inspiration and shows that you're not alone: You have love and guidance in the Holy Spirit! "The Lord himself goes before you and will be with you; He will never leave you," (Deuteronomy 31:8).

I also believe *location* is key to opening a successful business with God's guidance. He will show you where that location is. He showed me a shopping center in an area where there's plenty of traffic and parking space! It's important for your business to be visible from all directions.

Next, it is vital to negotiate a good lease, preferably 10 years, so you have enough time for success. If possible, I would purchase a business that is not doing well, that way you can get it at a discount. Then, do some minor cosmetic touchups. Buy some new equipment that you might need to make the place look clean and beautiful. During this while process, pray that God would be involved. Ask for His wisdom and knowledge and He will show you what to do! Keep God first and you will be successful!

Next, establish a corporation. Decide on a proper name for your business, go to your local bank, set up a business banking account, and get yourself a good accountant. Go apply for a food establishment permit. You can do this at your county health department. Find good vendors such as restaurant suppliers where you can get ingredients such as flour, pizza sauces, mozzarella cheese, and all kinds of toppings for your pizza. Contact soda vendors, pizza box companies, and seek out the best quality ingredients. Soon you'll be on your way!

"The Lord will send a blessing on your barns and on everything you put your hand to. The Lord your God will bless you in the land he is giving you."

Deuteronomy 28:8

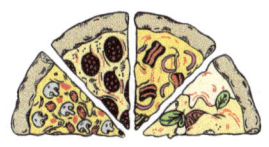

CHAPTER V:

SEEK GOD'S ADVICE IN EVERY SITUATION!

I just want you to know that if you truly seek God's will for your business, He will speak to you in a small voice and help you decide which way to go in every situation. When you open your business, always be polite, courteous, and give the best that you have! Give it your all! This is what God wants from you. I know you will be successful. When you have the power of God behind you, don't forget to give back to others. Give back to your community, give back to God, and be sure to thank Him every day of your life for the things He has given you.

Owning a small business is no easy task. You have ups and downs. It's what you do when you're down that makes the ups so much better! In my experience, in this business you'll do long hours. You will be away from your family. If it's possible, involve your family in every aspect. When

GOD AND PIZZA

I was running my pizzeria, I involved my children, and it made me feel proud to have them there with me. I can show them how a business is run, just as my father showed me. Amazing things happen when you involve God in your business, your family, and your life. He fills it with love, happiness, and peace, so please always seeks God's will in your life.

> *"You will seek me and find me when you seek me with all your heart."*
> **Jeremiah 29:13**

CHAPTER VI:

ALWAYS PLEASE GOD AND SET GOALS!

When I play Christian music at my pizzeria and sing praises to our Lord Jesus Christ, I know He is pleased with me! Psalms 95:2 says, "Let us come before him in thanksgiving and extol him with music and songs!" Take the time to stop, listen to the music, and sing along in praise and glory. Say a little prayer (especially when it's a hectic day) for peace and understanding for what is going on at that moment. It really helps you to focus and concentrate!

You must set goals for life and for your business. These can be short-term and long-term goals. Short-term goals can be setting up an advertisement for your business, bringing more sales, seeing weekly growth, or simply taking care of customers so they appreciate the service that you provide. Long-term goals can be where you want your business to go in the future, how much growth that you see for that business, or what will it take to get there! My father always told me to treat people with respect because not only is it the right thing to do, but you will be treated with respect also. When you're dealing with your vendors, suppliers, customers, or even your workers, be sure to always treat them with respect and patience!

> *"And without faith it is impossible to please God, because anyone that comes to Him must believe that He exists and that He rewards those who earnestly seek Him."*
> **Hebrews 11:6**

CHAPTER VII:

YOU WILL HAVE YOUR UPS AND DOWNS!

In your life and in your business, you will have ups and downs! It's how you handle the downs that makes the ups so special!

When I first opened my new pizzeria in 2015, things started a little slow. I was doing all the right things to get it started. I was praying every day and giving thanks to our Lord Jesus Christ. I was using the best ingredients, doing local advertising, greeting customers, and giving it my all!

Eventually, we started seeing an increase in sales and great comments on our service and food. Customers loved the praise music and commented on how they felt the presence of the Holy Spirit while enjoying a delicious meal. That made me feel amazing, and I thanked God for it all. By the end of 2019, we had the best sales yet!

Then, COVID-19 hit, and all businesses closed. I couldn't understand what was happening. Everything was going so great, I felt truly blessed, then suddenly I was losing everything again. However, I thought to myself, "You know what? This time I trust in God!" Yes, I was concerned, but I was not worried because I knew this time God had my back. I had been praying every day, worshiping Jesus, thanking God for my business, asking Him to protect it and let nothing hurt it. Even though my income was cut in half, and I had a hard time paying my mortgage, I wasn't worried. I had faith in God and trust in Jesus. I knew this was temporary! God promised me double for my trouble!

The power of prayer is amazing. I continued to give God the glory. I continued to praise His name and thank Him for all he had given me so far. The following year, all the business we lost during the pandemic came back. The next year, that business doubled, then *tripled*! Every day I fall on my knees and thank God and my Lord Jesus for His blessings. This is why I believe that how you handle your "down" season will make your "up" season double or triple times better. In times of trouble and worry, sit still and let God do His work in your life. Besides, how much can you add to your life by worrying?

"Anxiety weighs down the heart, but a kind word cheers it up."
Proverbs 12:25

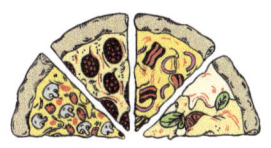

CHAPTER VIII:

THANKING GOD AND GIVING BACK!

I can't say enough about the power of prayer. It is so important to pray for God's protection against anything that will come against your business, family, friends, and customers. Always give thanks for all that He has given you. Jesus loves you. He only wants good for you and your success, happiness and peace. You will achieve these things when you pray and praise His holy name!

Then, when you are successful, give back. Help others with their miracle. I remember one day when I was working a man came in and said, "Hi, my name is Chris. I live in Utah, and I am thinking about opening a pizzeria!" I asked him if he had a plan yet. He had a location but had no idea how to get started. I told him that if he ever needs advice to give me a call and I would be happy to help. I thought to myself, *that's great, I hope he succeeds!* About a week later, Chris gave me a call. "What can I do for you?" I asked. I wanted to help him in every way I could. Chris said that he would like for me to show him how to get started in the pizza business. He wanted to fly me to Utah for a few days to show him the ropes! To make a long story short, I went to Utah. I met his lovely family. He insisted on putting me in a hotel and wanted to help me in every way he could. He was so grateful, and it felt so good to help a brother in need. We are good friends to this day, and his pizzeria is thriving!

It is so important to give back. You can do this through hosting a charity event, feeding the homeless, or giving back to your local church. This will put a smile on God's face, and when He smiles down on you, miracles happen. When I started giving back, I started feeling a sense of peace and joy. I knew God was smiling down on me.

I'm saying all of this because I've lived it. I've seen my business fail when I didn't pray and put God first. When I saw the light and realized it's not about me; it's about having faith, hope, and love in Jesus, that's when my miracle happened. I want your miracle to happen, too. I dedicate my life and business to the Lord Jesus Christ every day, and that has changed my life forever.

"Always giving thanks to God the Father for everything, in the name of our Lord Jesus Christ!"
Ephesians 5:20

CHAPTER IX:

REMEMBERING WHAT GOD HAS DONE FOR YOU!

It's very important not to forget what God has done and all the good things He has given you. He is your Father in heaven, he is there to love you, to care for you, and to guide you. That's why he sacrificed His only begotten son Jesus and resurrected Him from the grave, so that we may have the Holy Spirit; our counselor to be with us and guide us always. Just like our own mothers and fathers here on earth, we can call to Jesus, and he sends the Holy Spirit to protect and guide us.

Never forget where you came from. My father taught me hard work, how to make pizza, and how to run a business. My mother taught me love and compassion for others, recipes for Italian sauces, and the secret to making fresh pasta. With her amazing lasagna and love for cooking, she always wanted to be hands-on. My mom knew how to make pizza when most women didn't cook in restaurants, and she did it better than anyone. It was amazing watching her spin a pizza! She would stretch the dough in a round circle, then put a ladle of sauce in the center, moving it in a circular motion right to the edge of the crust. Then she would spread mozzarella cheese all over the pizza and slide it right into the oven. That was the best-tasting pizza I ever ate because it was made with my mother's love. I remember as a boy waking up on Sunday mornings to the delicious aroma of her cooking and the sound of garlic and onions sizzling in olive oil. That was the best way to wake up in the morning. I don't know how she did it, but she would still have the time to make me blueberry pancakes before we went to church. Then when we came back home, we would enjoy her fresh pasta, complete with Italian tomato sauce, grated Romano cheese, and fresh Italian crispy bread. Those are the memories that I will never forget.

My mom is no longer with us, she has gone to be with the Lord. I know she is in heaven with a seat at the Lord's table, cooking up a big pot of fresh pasta and tomato sauce and smiling down on me and my success. I love you and miss you, Mama. I know we will meet again!

So, when I say don't forget what God has done for you, I mean thank Him every day. Tell God about when He helped you to see the light and how He was there for you in the darkest times. Don't forget the fond memories of the past, the good times of your childhood. I guarantee it will put a big smile on your face.

REMEMBERING WHAT GOD HAS DONE FOR YOU!

"Remember the wonders He has done, his miracles, and the judgments He pronounced."
Psalms 105:5

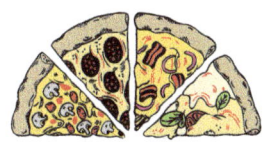

CHAPTER X:

LET THEM EAT WITH THEIR EYES!

The term "eat with your eyes" describes the feeling you get when the food you're about to eat looks so delicious that your mouth starts watering. When my mom cooked Sunday mornings, the sight, the sound, the smell… It lit up all my senses and made my mouth water.

So, when I built my pizzeria, I put up a 10-foot glass showcase so I could display all the wonderful and delicious pizzas I would be creating. When my customers would see them, their mouths would literally water! Right away, the sight, sounds, and smells would grab them, and they couldn't wait to get their favorite slice of pizza.

A few of my delicious pizzas are:

Traditional Cheese Pizza!

Sicilian Deep-dish Pizza!

Margarita Pizza!

Gramma Thin Crust Pizza!

I make a few gourmet-style pizzas as well:

Greek Salad Pizza with a Garlic Bread Crust!

Chicken Parmigiana Pizza!

Eggplant Parmigiana Pizza!

BBQ Chicken Pizza!

Brooklyn Style Pizza!

Each of these are served by the slice, or able to be purchased as a whole pizza.

I believe my glass showcase is the stage, and my pizzas are the actors getting ready for the big performance. Everything must be neat and clean for the presentation. Then, I open the doors and the audience comes in to try my wonderful and delicious pizzas!

I truly believe this is God's destiny for my life. I find myself being very creative coming up with new pizza ideas. I thank Him every day for the skill and the energy He has given me and the love for cooking He gave my mom that rubbed off on me.

Now I focus on giving back to others, especially my children. The gift of knowing God and that He gave His only son Jesus Christ to be sacrificed for our sins is the first

LET THEM EAT WITH THEIR EYES!

thing they should know and believe. Then, I'll teach them all about the pizza business as my father taught me. This will help them interact with others and have a good work ethic.

"So, whether you eat or drink or whatever you do, do it all for the glory of God."
1 Corinthians 10:31

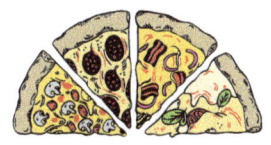

CHAPTER XI:

TEACHING THE NEXT GENERATION!

I am so grateful that my father taught me everything there is to know about the pizza business. Yes, he was hard on me, but you know what, I'm a better man for it! That's why it's so important to teach my children not only about the business, but about life. I had my children come work with me when they were younger, teaching them things like washing dishes, sweeping, and moping. They learned how to serve customers, work the cash register, and give change. This gave them good work ethics and life skills. I loved having them with me at work, those are some of the fondest memories of my life.

I also started teaching them about God and Jesus, how God sent his only begotten Son to be born from the Virgin Mary. I told them about the life Jesus lived, the miracles He performed, and the sacrifice He made to forgive all of us of our sins. I reminded them to read the Bible and take in God's word, to trust in Him, worship Him, and give Him all the glory.

I believe it is so important to pass down what we learn in life to our children. Now, my children are older. My son Joseph worked with me for a while and eventually decided to pursue his own career and is doing well. My daughter Marissa is going to the Culinary Arts Institute to become a chef and wants to open her own restaurant one day. I know God has a plan for both of them, so I do my part by praying for God's guidance, love, safety, and blessings to come upon them. I know the love that they have for God will guide them, that He will give them strength, wisdom, knowledge, and help them achieve all their hopes and dreams. My children are God-loving, Jesus-worshiping children of the highest God. I know God is smiling down on them. Because I love my children, I taught them that Jesus loves them and that He is there for them in every situation. I taught them how they can have a personal relationship with Jesus, and that if they can give up their worries and burdens to Him, they will have peace and joy in their lives!

> *"Tell it to your children, and let your children tell it to their children, and their children to the next generation."*
> **Joel 1:3**

CHAPTER XII:

HAVE PATIENCE WITH GOD AND PEOPLE!

It's so important to have patience! But it's also easy to lose your patience. Especially with dissatisfied customers, which you will get! You can't please everyone— that's another thing my father taught me. But you can always stay calm and make it right. Offer something for free or a credit for next time they come in. Even though they came in dissatisfied, they can leave satisfied because you did not lose your patience. Pray for these customers; they might be having a bad day. By showing your patience and understanding you will act like Jesus. Show compassion and shine his light onto others!

Ask God to give you patience and He will; He's a loving God!

Sometimes, you may want to lose your patience with your employees. Maybe they do something wrong, or they struggle to do things the way you want them done. Just stop for a moment, think about the situation, and then calmly resolve the problem. You will feel better that you did!

You may lose your patience sometimes, but remember that because of God's love inside you, you can resolve the problem and move on.

Sometimes, you may lose your patience with God. Maybe you prayed for more business or the health and wellbeing for a loved one, but God hasn't answered you yet.

Have patience with God; He works in His time, not yours! I believe if you ask God for something and then you worry and dwell on it every day, you're not letting God do His work. It's like God is saying, "I guess you got this, I will just step back and let you deal with it! I love you I will wait for you!" But if you ask in Jesus' name, fall on your knees, and let it go and give up, God will say "Okay, I will go to work for you, my child!" He will send out an angel army to work on your burdens and troubles. Then watch the miracle happen in His time!

So again, the power of prayer is amazing, and it is so important to pray for patience and to love others as He has loved you. When you do this, you will learn to have patience for others!

"My command is this: Love each other as I have loved you."
John 15:12

CHAPTER XIII:

FIND TIME TO MAKE GOD AND YOURSELF HAPPY!

When you have succeeded in your career, pray to God for time to enjoy life! God will truly bless you when you pray for your business and your family.

Remember what my father taught me: Teach someone else that job so you can move on to the next one!

Teach your children or an employee how to operate the business so you can have time off and take a well-deserved vacation. Give yourself alone time with God. Catch up on your reading of the Word, it develops a strong bond with Him! You will find He has more for you to do.

Consider doing more for your community, such as feeding people experiencing homelessness. Maybe take mission trips to other countries to help spread the gospel of our Lord Jesus Christ. There is no better way to show love like sharing the gospel. Let people know that Jesus loves them and that if they truly believe that he sacrificed himself on the cross they will be forgiven of their sins!

That will change their lives forever and you will have so much peace and joy in your life.

One thing God has put on my heart for when I retire is to set up kitchens in areas where there are those who are less fortunate. I would like to put up tents and install ovens, refrigerators, and prep stations to prepare food for as many people as possible! I pray every day for God to send me the resources to make this happen.

I know it's God speaking to me because the thought of it runs through my mind repeatedly. He tells me how to build and set up the kitchen in almost full detail. How can I not say that's God speaking to me? It just feels so right!

I can only imagine the day when my time comes to leave this earth; when I stand in the presence of Jesus Christ who will say, "Well done my good and faithful servant." I'll receive a big hug and kiss as he says, "Welcome to Heaven." Then, I'll be greeted by my mom and all my past relatives. I can't wait to stand in the presence of God and hear the thousands upon thousands of holy angels singing praises to the Lord! Oh, what a glorious day that will be!

I give glory, honor, power, and praise to you my Lord Jesus Christ, my savior, my redeemer, my Rock, my cornerstone! It's you that gave me the strength, wisdom, and knowledge to achieve all the things in my life!

Hallelujah, Hallelujah, Hallelujah! Amen.

*"I can do all this through him
who gives me strength!"*
Philippians 4:13

*"Call to me and I will answer you and tell
you great and unsearchable things you do
not know!"*
Jeremiah 33:3

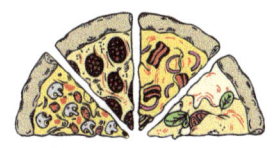

CHAPTER XIV

CONCLUSION: BE GRATEFUL

Being grateful is so important to God! Be grateful for all He has done for you, like giving you the skills, wisdom, knowledge, and drive to accomplish all that you have done. Be grateful. I cannot stress it enough! Be grateful for all He has done for you.

When you become successful in your business you will feel on top of the world. Please check yourself and remember that God guided you every step of the way! Tell Him how much you appreciate what He has done for you.

Be grateful! When you can feed your family, be grateful! When you can buy your dream house, be grateful! When you can send your kids to college, be grateful! When you can afford all the necessities for life, be grateful!

God has a plan for each of us. It's our goal in life to find out what that might be. What is your God-given talent?

What is it that you enjoy doing? Ask yourself what you should be doing with your life.

Pray to your Father in heaven. Be persistent and ask for guidance, wisdom, and understanding!

He will show you the way if you have the patience to let Him.

IN JESUS' NAME!

CHAPTER XV
A BUSINESS PLAN

A business plan can be defined as a guide, a blueprint, or a step-by-step process on how to start a business or company in any field. In retail, it could be selling clothing or antiques. In the food industry, it could be a coffee or a sandwich shop. It could even be a pizzeria. Whatever it is, you should start with a business plan!

Mine happened to be the pizza business. Here are ten tips to give you an idea on what this might look like:

TIPS

1. Know what kind of business you would like to be in! What are you good at doing? What is your God-given talent? Mine is the love for cooking and pizza!

2. Have your finances in order to purchase an existing business. You can also apply for a business loan.

3. Go search for that perfect location or that right

business! Pray for God's guidance to lead you to it. He will!

4. Once you find that business or location, you will need to either speak with the owner and negotiate a price or talk to the landlord about leasing that location.

5. Now get yourself a lawyer to look over the lease and make sure all the wording is correct. They will watch over your best interest! Request a five-year lease with the option for five more years so you're not locked into a long lease.

6. Go find a good accounting firm. They can help you get a corporation and register the name of your business. The name of your business is very important as it defines who you are and what you are selling. They will also help you set up sales tax payments and payroll for your employees.

7. If you're opening a food establishment, go to the local health department and apply for a food permit. Then schedule a final inspection for sanitation cleanliness and proper set up of hand sinks. They also can give you a list of the proper procedures to pass your inspection.

8. Now you need to check your equipment to make sure it is working properly! Check your refrigerators, freezers, ovens, dough mixers, stoves, and pizza ovens.

9. When you feel you have everything in order and all your boxes are checked, you're ready to start

preparing all your ingredients to make pizza and anything else that you would like to sell!

10. Remember to ask Jesus to be with you every step of the way. Pray as you put your business together. Ask Jesus to give you strength, ambition, and drive to accomplish your goals in getting your business open and ready to serve customers. Ask in Jesus' name and he will give it to you.

In the next chapter, I'll give you pizza recipes to help you get started if you choose the pizza business, or just to have and enjoy with family and friends. May God bless you and keep you in his favor! Glory to the highest in the name of our Lord Jesus Christ!

CHAPTER XVI
PIZZA RECIPES

These pizza recipes are traditional styles you can find in almost any pizza restaurant. The following are some of my most creative pizza recipes!

PIZZA DOUGH

3 cups bread flour (separate, use as needed)
1 cup warm water
1 tbs active dry yeast
1 tbs brown sugar
1/2 tsp salt
2 tbs olive oil

1. Combine 2 cups of bread flour, warm water, yeast, sugar, and salt in a bowl with an electric mixer fitted with a dough hook attachment.
2. Mix on low speed until blended but still moist, about 2 minutes. Cover bowl with towel and let rise in warm place until dough has doubled in size, about 20 minutes.
3. Uncover the bowl and mix with electric mixer on low speed until dough has come together, about 5 minutes. Sprinkle in the remaining flour a little at a time until soft, sticky dough forms, 1-2 minutes. Do not over-flour your dough.
4. Increase mixer speed to medium and mix until dough pulls away from side of bowl, about 8 minutes. Cover bowl with towel and let rest about 20 minutes.
5. Rub olive oil evenly into a plastic container.
6. Transfer dough onto a floured work surface. Dust hands with flour and knead dough until soft but still wet on the inside. Form into a ball and place in oiled container, cover, and store in refrigerator for at least 1 day and up to 7 days.

Tips:

All the flour may not be needed. Aim for a soft, sticky dough. This recipe can make 2 12-inch pizzas or 1 16-inch pizza.

PIZZA SAUCE

6 oz can of tomato paste
30 oz can of tomato sauce
2-4 tbs dried oregano (to taste)
2-4 leaves of fresh basil chopped
8 oz of grated pecorino Romano cheese
1 tbs salt
1/2 tsp black pepper
2 tsp sugar

1. Mix tomato paste and tomato sauce in a medium bowl until smooth.
2. Add the rest of the ingredients (oregano, salt, black pepper, sugar, fresh basil, and pecorino Romano cheese) into bowl and mix until well blended.
3. Taste and adjust seasoning to your liking.

Sauce blend can make three 12-inch pizzas or two 16-inch.

Tips:
You want to have a thick pizza sauce; you can add water to thin out your sauce but don't add too much.

CHEESES

There are many kinds of cheeses out there to choose from! You have hard cheeses such as pecorino Romano, parmigiana regatta, and ricotta ensalada, and soft melting cheeses such as fresh mozzarella, aged mozzarella, smoked mozzarella, provolone, and cheddar. Anyone of these are good toppings for your pizza, depending on your taste. Any combination of two or three of them works great, too!

Use your imagination and be creative. A pizza is like a blank canvas. Use your ingredients like an artist uses their paint. Design a work of art and have fun putting the pizza together.

THE NEAPOLITIAN CHEESE PIZZA

1 prepared dough ball
1- 10 oz ladle of pizza sauce
1 lb. of shredded mozzarella cheese
1 tbs of olive oil
1 cup of flour

1. Take your fresh dough ball out of refrigerator and set it aside for 30 minutes.
2. Prepare a workspace by spreading a small amount of olive oil in a circle.
3. Place dough ball in the center of olive oil. Spread it and start to press down with fingertips constantly in a circular pattern.
4. Once you've achieved the perfect size and shape, make sure your dough is an even 16-inch circle!
5. Apply a half of a handful of flour and spread it around the dough. Though not required, it would be great if you have a 16-inch pizza stone to place in your oven pre-heated to 425 degrees.
6. Turn a 16-inch aluminum pizza pan upside down and apply a little flour to bottom. Pick up the flattened dough ball and put the floured side down onto the pizza pan. Stretch it to fit the size of the pan to make sure the dough ball can slide freely.
7. Sprinkle a small handful of mozzarella onto dough and slide onto a pre-heated pizza stone.
8. Precook dough for 5 minutes, then take it out of oven.
9. Add a 10-ounce ladle full of pizza sauce to your dough and spread it out in a circular motion until the sauce is about 1 inch from the edge of the dough.
10. Now you can start adding your mozzarella cheese. Spread it on top of the sauce until it is covered to the edge!
11. Open oven and carefully slide your pizza back on top of the pizza stone, making sure it slides off the pizza pan. If you don't have a pizza stone, you can place your flattened pizza dough on an oiled right-side up aluminum pizza pan and place it in middle rack of your pre-heated oven!
12. Cook at 425 degrees for 10 to 15 minutes, turning the pizza after 5 minutes of cooking. Cook until the crust is golden brown and the cheese is bubbly!
13. Take pizza out of oven, let it cool, and cut it into 8 slices.
14. Enjoy your very own home-made cheese pizza!

THE MARGARITA PIZZA

1 dough ball (1 to 2 lbs.)
1- 16 oz can of whole plum tomatoes
1 lb. of fresh mozzarella cheese
1/2 cup of grated pecorino Romano cheese
2 oz of extra virgin olive oil
6 leaves of fresh basil
Salt and pepper (to taste)

1. On an oiled surface, press the dough ball with your fingertips into a 16-inch circle. Sprinkle flour on top and spread evenly.
2. Use the same method as the cheese pizza. Preheat oven to 425 degrees and slide the pizza onto the preheated pizza stone!
3. Prebake for 5 minutes.
4. Take out of the oven and place slices of fresh mozzarella on top of prebaked pizza crust.
5. Open the can of tomatoes and drain the liquid. Crush tomatoes in a small bowl and remove excess liquid. Place crushed tomatoes on top of pizza, but do not cover completely.
6. Add salt and pepper to taste. Then add a half of a hand full of grated Romano cheese on top and drizzle with extra virgin olive oil.
7. Place pizza back into oven on top of pizza stone and bake additional 10 minutes or until the crust is golden brown and the cheese is bubbly.
8. Take pizza out of the oven and cut it into 8 slices. Tear fresh basil leaves and place them on top of your beautiful margarita pizza. ENJOY!

THE SICILIAN PIZZA

1 dough ball (2-3 lbs.) double original dough recipe
1-16x10 rectangular pizza pan
1- 10 oz ladle of pizza sauce
1 1/2 lbs. of shredded mozzarella cheese
1 tbs vegetable shortening
1/2 tsp oregano
2 tbs of parmigiana regatta
Drizzle of extra virgin olive oil

ASSEMBLING THE SICILLIAN PIZZA

1. Take your prepared dough ball out of refrigerator let stand 30 minutes. Meanwhile, preheat your oven to 425 degrees.
2. Take the rectangular pan and coat with vegetable shortening. Place your dough ball on work surface and begin to press down in a rectangular shape, pulling on corners to form.
3. Spread a small amount of olive oil on to dough evenly.
4. Using three fingers, create dimples up and down the dough.
5. Wrap with one sheet of plastic wrap and let stand in a warm area until it doubles in size.
6. Once pizza crust is ready, spread 10 ounces of pizza sauce evenly on crust, leaving a one-inch border.
7. Spread the shredded mozzarella on top of sauce until covered.
8. Sprinkle the oregano and parmigiana on top of pizza, drizzle with remaining olive oil, and place on middle rack of oven.
9. Bake for 15-20 minutes until crust is golden brown and cheese is bubbly.
10. Let pizza cool and cut into 8 slices.
11. Enjoy your Sicilian pizza!

THE TOMATO PESTO PIZZA

1 dough ball (2-3 lbs. double original dough recipe)
16x10 rectangle pizza pan
10 fresh ripe plum tomatoes (chopped)
1 lb. of fresh mozzarella
2 cloves of garlic (chopped)
1/4 cup extra virgin olive oil
1 tsp of oregano
Salt and pepper to taste

In a bowl, mix chopped tomatoes, garlic, oregano, salt, pepper and olive oil.

PESTO SAUCE

2 bunches of fresh basil (about 30 leaves or so)
1 cup extra virgin olive oil
2-3 cloves of garlic
2 tbs of toasted pine nuts
8 oz of grated parmigiana cheese
Salt and pepper to taste

PESTO SAUCE DIRECTIONS

1. In a blender, mix basil leaves, garlic, toasted pine nuts, parmigiana cheese, salt, and pepper.
2. Add half the amount of olive oil and blend.
3. Drizzle in remaining oil until smooth.

ASSEMBLING THE TOMATO PESTO PIZZA

1. Use instructions from Sicilian pizza recipe for dough ball and pizza pan.
2. Once you stretch dough onto pan and brush olive oil on top, cover with plastic wrap.
3. Let rise.
4. Remover plastic wrap and press dough down with fingers to release air that has formed.
5. Cover with plastic wrap and let rise a second time.
6. When risen, remove plastic wrap and place in 425-degree oven.
7. After 5 minutes, remove from oven and cover the top of pizza with one layer of fresh mozzarella. Add the chopped tomatoes on top and drizzle with pesto sauce. Add remaining mozzarella.
8. Place back into oven and bake additional 20–25 minutes. Cook until golden brown and cheese is bubbly. Garnish top with chopped tomatoes and chopped fresh basil.
9. Enjoy your tomato pesto pizza!

THE CHICKEN PARMIGIANA PIZZA

1 prepared dough ball (1-2 lbs.)
6 chicken tenders (cut into cube size pieces)
10 oz of prepared pizza sauce
10 oz of grated parmigiana cheese
1 cup of ricotta cheese
1 1/2 lbs. of shredded mozzarella cheese
1 cup of flour
1 cup buttermilk
Salt and pepper
4 oz olive oil
1 16-inch round pizza pan

PREPARING THE CHICKEN

1. Place chicken tender cubes into a bowl and add butter milk.
2. Season with salt and pepper, mix, and cover with plastic wrap.
3. Place chicken into refrigerator.
4. After 1 hour, take chicken out of refrigerator and drain buttermilk.
5. In a clean bowl, mix flour and a pinch of salt and pepper.
6. Add chicken pieces and toss until well-coated.
7. Place frying pan on stovetop. Set to medium-high heat and add olive oil.
8. Fry chicken until golden brown.
9. Once chicken is done, drain excess oil onto paper towel and set aside.

ASSEMBLING THE CHICKEN PARMESANA PIZZA

1. Preheat oven to 425 degrees.
2. On a work surface, add a small amount of olive oil in a circle. Place prepared dough ball in center. Work dough into a circle.
3. Lightly coat 16-inch pizza pan with olive oil. Place round pizza dough on pan, making sure dough is spread all the way to the edge.
4. Spread a half pound of shredded mozzarella on top of dough and place into preheated oven.
5. After 5 minutes, take pizza out of oven and add the 10 ounces of pizza sauce in a circular motion.
6. Spread prepared chicken evenly on top of pizza.
7. In a small bowl, add ricotta cheese, a pinch of salt and pepper, and 1 tablespoon of grated parmesan. Mix well.
8. Scatter ricotta cheese mixture one teaspoon at a time on pizza surface. Top pizza with remaining mozzarella and parmesan cheese.
9. Place pizza back into oven and cook for additional 10 to 15 minutes until golden brown and bubbly.
10. Take pizza out of oven and let cool. Cut into 8 slices and enjoy your chicken parmigiana pizza!

THE EGGPLANT PARMIGIANA PIZZA

2 medium-sized eggplants, cut 1/4 in. (preferably Sicilian eggplant)
3 eggs
2 cups of flour
3 cups seasoned breadcrumbs
1 prepared dough ball
10 oz prepared pizza sauce
10 oz grated parmigiana cheese.
1 1/2 lbs. of shredded mozzarella cheese
1 cup ricotta cheese
2 cups canola oil
4 oz olive oil
Salt and pepper
16-inch pizza pan
3 bowls

PREPARING THE EGGPLANT

1. Remove outer skin of eggplant and slice into ¼ inch slices.
2. In bowl #1, add flour and add a pinch of salt and pepper.
3. In bowl #2, add three eggs and a pinch of salt and pepper. Whisk until blended.
4. In bowl #3, add seasoned breadcrumbs.
5. Add canola oil to a frying pan. Place on stovetop on medium heat.
6. Equally coat slices of eggplant in order of bowls (#1, #2, then #3). Repeat process for each slice of eggplant.
7. Increase heat of frying pan to 350-375 degrees. Fry eggplant slices carefully until golden brown.
8. Once eggplant is cooked, place on paper towel to absorb excess oil.

ASSEMBLING THE EGGPLANT PARMIGIANA PIZZA

1. Preheat oven to 425 degrees. On a work surface, spread a little olive oil in a circle, place dough ball, and press into a circle.
2. Coat pizza pan with a little olive oil and place dough ball. Make sure dough reaches the edge of pan. Spread 1/2 pound of mozzarella on dough and place into preheated oven.
3. After 5 minutes, take pizza crust out of oven and spread sauce up to edge of dough, leaving a one-inch crust. Place prepared eggplant slices on top of pizza until covered.
4. Place ricotta cheese, a pinch of salt and pepper, and two pinches of parmesan cheese into a small bowl and mix well.
5. Spread ricotta mixture on top of pizza in teaspoon-sized dots. Cover pizza with remaining mozzarella and parmesan cheese.
6. Return to oven and continue to cook for an additional 10–15 minutes until crust is golden brown and cheese is bubbly.
7. Take out of oven, let cool, and cut into 8 equal pieces.
8. Enjoy your eggplant parmigiana pizza!

THE BROOKLYN PIZZA

1 prepared pizza dough (1 to 2 lbs.)
16 x 10 rectangle pizza pan
1 tbs of vegetable shortening
1 – 16 oz can crush tomatoes
3 fresh basil leaves
2 garlic cloves sliced thin
8 oz of olive oil
Salt and pepper
1/4 tsp red pepper flakes
1/2 tsp oregano
8 oz parmesan cheese
2 lbs. of shredded mozzarella cheese

PREPARING THE SAUCE

1. In a medium-sized sauce pot, add olive oil and heat on stove top.
2. Add the garlic, salt, pepper, and red pepper flakes.
3. Sautee until garlic is light brown.
4. Add the crushed tomatoes and basil leaves. Heat until bubbly then reduce heat to simmer and cook additional 20 minutes.
5. Let sauce cool.

ASSEMBLING THE BROOKLYN PIZZA

1. Coat rectangle pizza pan with vegetable shortening, making sure to coat the sides.
2. On a work surface, begin to stretch prepared pizza dough in a rectangle.
3. Place pizza dough onto pan and spread evenly to the edge, pressing dough to sides to form a crust.
4. Brush olive oil to cover pizza dough and seal top with plastic wrap. Let rise in warm area until size doubles.
5. When the pizza dough has risen, remove plastic wrap and pinch the edges to form the crust. With your fingertips, press down on dough to form dimples. Spread shredded mozzarella on top of pizza and place into 450-degree oven for 5-10 minutes until cheese starts to brown.
6. Take pizza out of oven and evenly spread prepared sauce on top of pizza until covered. Sprinkle oregano, parmesan cheese, and olive oil on top of pizza and return to oven.
7. Cook for additional 15-20 minutes until crust is golden brown and sauce is bubbly.
8. Take out of oven, let cool, and cut into 8 slices.
9. Enjoy your Brooklyn pizza!

CONCLUSION

My story and how important it is to accept Jesus Christ as our Lord and savior inspired me to write *GOD and PIZZA*. It is so important that we ask God to guide everything in our lives from our hopes and dreams to our businesses. We can have faith and trust that He will lead us on the right path. God will use the least of us to accomplish the most. I mean, look at me! I dropped out of high school, never went to college, and later went on to get my GED. Today, I am a successful entrepreneur in business and in life. I truly believe if you work hard enough to accomplish your dreams and let God lead the way, He will be there for you.

It's important not to stress if it takes too long for your dreams to become a reality. You must let God work. I believe the more you stress and say to yourself, "Why is it taking so long? Why hasn't my dream come to pass?" God will step back and say, "Well if you want to worry and not trust in me, then I will love you and let you figure it out yourself." All you need to do is have faith the size of a mustard seed, be still, let God do His work, and submit yourself to His will for your life. You will be amazed on what He can help you accomplish in your business.

When I was in Florida and that amazing family introduced me to Christianity, I was like the seed that was sown along the path where birds came and ate them up in Matthew 13. I heard the message but didn't fully understand, so the evil one stole what was planted in my heart. When I came back to New York to take over my father's business and started attending church again, I became the seed that fell among the thorns. The seed grew, but the thorns choked the plant, and it shriveled up and died. I heard and understood the word, praised God, then let the troubles and worries of this world like success and money choke the love for God out of me. After we sold my father's business, I repented and asked God to forgive me of my transgressions. I became the seed that fell on good soil. I started understanding God's Word and eventually produced a good crop yielding a hundred times what was sown.

My life is successful because I repented. Today, I have a personal relationship with my Lord Jesus Christ. I don't do anything without praying to him first. The power of prayer is so amazing, and so are the blessings that come when you ask in his name and give Jesus Christ all the glory. To be saved is simple; you must believe that Jesus Christ was born to be the living sacrifice for us, was crucified on the cross, and rose on the third day so we may be forgiven of our sins and have the Holy Spirit dwell among us. I hope you find this book useful and uplifting. I write with faith, hope, and love for *GOD and PIZZA*.

MAY GOD BLESS YOU AND KEEP YOU IN JESUS' NAME.

Printed in the USA
CPSIA information can be obtained
at www.ICGtesting.com
LVHW020825030924
789973LV00003B/29